MIDLOTHIAN PUBLIC LIBRARY

3 1614 001

P9-CCG-917

MIDLOTHIAN PUBLIC LIBRARY
14701 S. KENTON AVE.
MIDLOTHIAN, IL 60445

BAKER & TAYLOR

TAKING ACTION AGAINST

Gangs

Sarah Levete

New York

MIDLOTHIAN PUBLIC LIBRARY
14701 S. KENTON AVE.
MIDLOTHIAN, IL 60445

Published in 2010 by The Rosen Publishing Group Inc.
29 East 21st Street, New York, NY 10010

Copyright © 2010 Wayland/The Rosen Publishing Group, Inc.

All rights reserved. No part of this book may be reproduced
in any form without permission from the publisher, except
by a reviewer.

First Edition

Editors: Sarah Eason and Robyn Hardyman
Editor for Wayland: Katie Powell
Consultant: Jayne Wright
Designers: Paul Myerscough and Rob Norridge
Picture researcher: Maria Joannou

Library of Congress Cataloging-in-Publication Data

Levete, Sarah.
 Taking action against gangs / Sarah Levete. -- 1st ed.
    p. cm. -- (Taking action)
 Includes index.
 ISBN 978-1-4358-9666-6 (library binding)
 ISBN 978-1-4358-9668-0 (paperback)
 ISBN 978-1-61532-490-3 (6-pack)
 1. Gangs--Juvenile literature. 2. Knife fighting--Juvenile
literature. 3. Crime prevention--Juvenile literature. I. Title.
 HV6437.L48 2010
 364.106'6--dc22
                        2009027029

Photo Credits:
Cover photographs: Photolibrary.
Interior photographs: Corbis: Angela Catlin 27, Jon Naso/Star
Ledger 30, Luis Rivera/Reuters 12–13; Fotolia: Paty Cullen 39;
Istockphoto: Sascha Burkard 5, Wouter van Caspel 35, Julie
Masson Deshaies 19, Ben Else 24, Erics Photography 4, 18,
Juan Estey 29, Jamie Evans 23, Felix Mizioznikov 15, Ondo
Nguyen 25, Knud Nielsen 11, S.P. Rayner 16, Snowkoala 22,
Dean Turner 34; Photolibrary: 6–7, 9, I Love Images 42,
PYMCA/Giles Moberly 43; Rex Features: Image Source 14,
Keystone USA 36, Jen Lowery 41, Tony Sapiano 37, Tom
Watkins 28; Shutterstock: Benis Arapovic 2–3, Sascha Burkard
31, Sam Cornwell 10, Laurence Gough 40, Matthew Heald
44–45, Lucekkk 1, Dmitry Matrosov 8, Julia Pivovarova 32–33,
Jason Stitt 26, Tootles 20–21; Wayland Archive: 47

Manufactured in China
CPSIA Compliance Information: Batch #WAW0102YA: For Further Information
contact Rosen Publishing, New York, New York at 1-800-237-9932

CONTENTS

Chapter 1

What are gangs and knife crime?

A *gang* is the word used to describe a group of people. A group of friends at the movie theater may be called a gang, as may a group of classmates in the playground. These gangs are harmless—they are made up of people who are just enjoying themselves. However, today the term "gang" is generally used in a negative sense. It describes a group of people whose behavior is threatening, antisocial, and often violent.

Despite all the negative headlines about gangs, most groups of young people just want to have a good time and stay safe.

Knife crime

Knife crime is the term used to describe the offense of using a knife to threaten or harm someone else. Today, many young people carry knives. Many people think they need a knife for protection, but it can also be used against the person who is carrying it. Other people carry knives with the deliberate intention of threatening and harming others. Whatever the reason for carrying a knife, it often results in serious injury or even death.

Gangs and knife crime

It is not necessarily a crime to be in a gang, but any criminal act carried out by a member of any gang is illegal. In some countries, it is illegal to belong to certain gangs known by the police to be responsible for serious crimes.

Every year, terrible injuries and even deaths are caused by knife and gun crimes carried out by gangs. In the United Kingdom, gangs are often linked to knife crime. In the United States, gangs are usually linked to gun crime, possibly because it is easier to get hold of a gun there.

Some people believe that carrying a knife is less dangerous than carrying a gun. This is not true. There are serious consequences for carrying a knife, and in many situations, it is illegal. Even if someone uses a knife only to defend themself, they could still injure or kill someone. They would then be sent to prison, often for years.

In the United States, anyone over the age of 18 can buy a gun. In the United Kingdom, it is illegal to own a handgun unless you have a license.

TALK ABOUT

Imagine this scene: an elderly, frail woman is walking home carrying a shopping bag. She sees a group of young people gathered on a street corner.

✶ Do you think the woman feels relieved to see a friendly group of kids who will help her carry her shopping, or do you think she is frightened that the gang of young people will attack her?

✶ What would you think in that situation?

✶ Does a large group of young people always mean trouble?

✶ Do you consider your group of friends to be a gang?

Useful tool, deadly weapon

People have always used sharp objects as weapons in society, whether to kill animals for food, to protect themselves, or to attack others. Knives are important tools, used in cooking, woodwork, building, and many industries. Every kitchen has a selection of sharp knives, but on the street, these knives can turn into deadly weapons. Although kitchen knives are common household items, the injuries they cause can be horrific and in some circumstances fatal.

Against the law?

In the United States, each state has its own laws about buying and carrying knives. In general, it is legal to carry a pocketknife with a blade that folds away as long as the blade is not longer than 2 or 3 inches (5 or 7.5 centimeters), depending on the state. You cannot take a knife of any kind into a school. In the United Kingdom, it is illegal for a person under the age of 16 to buy a knife. However, it is legal for a person under the age of 16 to carry a foldaway knife, such as a penknife, if the blade is less than 5 inches (7.5 centimeters) long.

Kitchen knives are the most commonly used weapon by street gangs in the United Kingdom.

Is knife crime getting worse?

In some parts of the world, knives have become the most common street weapons. Many people who carry knives do so for self-defense, for protection if they are threatened or attacked. In reality, carrying a knife offers little protection, because the knife is often turned against the person carrying it.

Recently, the number of victims of knife crime in the United Kingdom has made headlines around the world, with the death of more than 30 teenagers from knife wounds in a 10-month period during 2007 alone. These deaths and the numerous stabbings that happen across the country lead many people to believe that knife crime is spiraling out of control. Others disagree and say that knife crime is actually falling.

Other weapons

Knives are the most common murder weapon in England and Wales. In the United States in 2005, however, the Bureau of Justice Statistics Crime Characteristics recorded that 55% of murders were committed with handguns, 16% with other types of guns, 14% with knives, 5% with blunt objects, and 11% with other weapons.

FACTS

According to a survey conducted by INTERVICT at Tilburg University in the Netherlands, 5.9% of Americans were victims of knife crime between 2000 and 2005. In the same period in the United Kingdom, 12.2% of the population were victims of knife crime.

Chapter 2

Different kinds of gang

Gangs have existed for years. Historically, groups of people joined together to steal food from others or to take their land. Gangs often form for protection, and gang members usually share lifestyles or interests.

American gangs

In the lawless "Wild West" of the United States in the 1800s, gangs of outlaws roamed the land. Later, groups of immigrants who arrived in the United States formed gangs to protect themselves against other, already established, immigrant gangs. In the early 1970s, gangs such as the Bloods and the Crips became common in American cities such as Los Angeles.

Some gangs are groups of bored youngsters, but others are highly organized and run complex criminal networks.

Fierce rivals

Today, there are over 300 different Bloods and Crips gangs in Los Angeles County alone, and they commit crimes such as murder, drug dealing, and robbery. The Bloods and Crips are fierce rivals but there is also fighting within the gangs themselves.

An identity

Gangs develop an identity to give their members a sense of belonging and to intimidate their rivals. They follow gang rules and have a distinct way of dressing. Tattoos, hand signs, and graffiti often signal membership.

Other gangs may just wear a certain style of clothing, such as bandanas or hooded tops (hoodies). These can look intimidating and they can help to hide a person's identity.

Rituals and rules

Some gangs have strict rules and if a gang member breaks a rule, other gang members often violently punish the so-called offender.

A new member is often required to carry out an act of violence to prove his or her commitment to a gang. He or she might be forced to mug someone else, or he or she may be beaten or attacked by other gang members. New female gang members are sometimes forced to have sex with other gang members. Going through such a "ritual joining" is supposed to make the new gang member feel bound to the gang, as if they have earned their place, but in reality, it humiliates people and makes them slaves to the gang leaders.

A new gang member may have to endure violent beatings, or give another member a beating to prove their worth.

TALK ABOUT

✷ **What do you think is the difference between a group of several people who shout at and attack local people and a well-organized gang?**

✷ **Do you think they are both types of gang?**

Street gangs

Some gangs are known as street gangs or crews. These gangs try to take "ownership" of a particular area called a turf or patch. Sometimes gangs "tag" an area, marking a building or wall with graffiti to show it is their turf.

Street gangs attack rival gangs who dare to enter their so-called territory. This often results in fights over territory called "turf wars." Gangs may use knives, guns, and beatings to attack rivals.

Some street gangs begin as groups of bored, aimless young people who gather in one area and then wander around the streets. These young people may find themselves without proper care and support from their families. They may not have a network of support or healthy role models to look to for guidance and direction. They may not set out to cause trouble, but with nothing to do, no money, no work, and perhaps fueled by anger and frustration at their situation, they end up smashing bus shelters, breaking into cars, and threatening innocent people.

Young people who belong to gangs might think that throwing stones, shouting at people, and spraying offensive graffiti is harmless because it doesn't directly hurt an individual. However, such behavior can be intimidating and frightening for people of all ages. In time, this loosely joined group of youths may become a more organized street gang.

Graffiti signals a gang's control over an area and sometimes it sends messages, challenging and threatening rival gangs.

Organized gangs

Some gangs have developed into sophisticated criminal operations, run by criminals who control their gang through fear and violence. These gangs are involved in crimes such as manufacturing illegal drugs, drug trafficking, kidnapping, and theft. They are usually headed by a select few. Organized gangs are ruthless toward anyone who crosses them, including gang members who disobey the rules or who try to leave the gang.

Burned-out cars are often a result of car theft by street gangs.

A global problem

Gangs exist in most countries in the world. From Jamaica to Japan, gangs terrorize and threaten innocent people and rival gangs. The effect of gang behavior in one country can also be felt in another country. For instance, Jamaican street gangs, known as Posses, formed in the city of Kingston in Jamaica in the 1970s. These gangs traded illegal drugs, kidnapped people from rich families, and murdered rival gang members. Today, the Posses may be responsible for trafficking up to one-fifth of the illegal drug cocaine in the United States.

FACTS

In the United States, there are about 20,000 violent street gangs, motorcycle gangs, and prison gangs. About 1 million members of these gangs are criminally active in the United States today.

Maras

Gangs called Maras Salvatrucha (Maras) terrorize people and commit violent crimes across South American countries and the United States. These gangs formed during a civil war that tore apart the South American country El Salvador in the early 1980s. To escape the devastation caused by the war, many people left the country and settled in Los Angeles, California. Here, they banded together in gangs to protect themselves from attack and intimidation from other gangs that were already established in the area. After carrying out beatings, murders, and kidnappings, members of the Maras were sent back by the United States authorities to El Salvador. There, the violence and criminal activity of the gangs spread to neighboring countries, including Honduras.

In Honduras in 2003, it became illegal to be a member of Maras. Even displaying a tattoo symbolizing gang membership can result in a 12-year prison sentence. However, this "zero tolerance" approach to gang membership means that Honduran prisons are now packed with gang members who continue to exert their violence and power in society, running their criminal activities from within the prison walls.

Prison gangs

In the Brazilian city of Sao Paulo, a group that began as a soccer team in a prison in 1993 developed into a powerful, violent gang whose influence terrorized prison inmates and spread well beyond the prison walls. The group is called the Primeiro Comando da Capital (PCC) and is responsible for running criminal activities such as drug trafficking and attacks against the police. The gang use cell phones to coordinate their activities outside the prison from inside the prison walls.

There are about 30,000 members of MS-13, a gang that belongs to the Maras Salvatrucha group. Members, both men and women, are brutally beaten when they join the gang. They often use machetes, knives with blades about 24 inches (60 centimeters) long, to attack their victims.

FACTS

There are several "outlaw" biker gangs, including the Hells
Angels. Membership of the Hells Angels is gained at various
stages: a person joins as a "supporter," and is then promoted to a
"hangaround" before becoming a "probationer." They finally
become a full member, voted in by members from the local branch.

Chapter 3

What do gangs do?

Gangs are sometimes involved in crime, from violent muggings to international drug trafficking. They often thrive on intimidating innocent people with threats and acts of violence. Local businesses may have to pay money to gangs to prevent them from attacking and ruining their business. If they don't pay, they run the risk of being brutally beaten or seeing their business burned down.

Gangs and drugs

Selling illegal drugs makes a lot of money. Gang members called runners deliver the drugs and collect the money from drug users. A few gang leaders get enormously rich by trading drugs, but most gang members do not. Instead, they face a life of danger on the streets from rival gangs and are at risk of being caught by the police and spending the rest of their lives in prison. Some people who are addicted to drugs, and whose drugs are supplied by a particular gang, may be forced into committing crimes in order to get the drugs they need.

Many gang members who deal in illegal drugs are themselves sometimes addicted to drugs.

Gang wars

Each gang wants to make money from the illegal drugs trade in a particular area, and there is much rivalry between them as they fight over their "turf" or territory. In the 1990s in Quebec, Canada, a "war" between the Hells Angels and the rival Rock Machine biker gang led to the death of 150 people. Recent attacks in the area have sparked fears that gangs are once again fighting for control over neighborhoods and criminal activity.

Mugging

Mugging is a violent robbery, usually in a public place. Muggers often work in gangs, threatening and injuring victims with knives, but some muggers work alone. Steaming is the slang term used in the U.K. to describe attacks made by several gang members on innocent people traveling by bus, train, or underground train. In these attacks, knives are often used to threaten victims in order to steal items such as cell phones, handbags, expensive watches, and MP3 players. The attackers usually make money from selling the items they have stolen. The money then often goes toward buying the gang members drugs or funding other illegal activities.

Muggers target innocent victims for any valuable goods or money they may carry.

FACTS

* According to the National Alliance of Gang Investigators Associations, gangs are the main distributors of drugs in the United States.

* The Federal Bureau of Investigation (FBI) estimates that the Hells Angels gang makes 1 billion dollars a year from the illegal drugs trade.

Who are the victims?

Anyone can be the victim of gang crime. Gangs often attack vulnerable people, such as senior citizens, who cannot run away or fight back. They may attack or mug them for a cell phone or for money. Sometimes individuals are targeted for a particular reason, such as challenging a gang member over his or her behavior. Sometimes people end up being attacked for something as trivial as staring at a gang member.

Wrong place, wrong time

Sometimes victims of gang violence are innocent passersby, who are unlucky enough to be in the wrong place at the wrong time. In 1995 in Los Angeles, a family driving home from a birthday party took a wrong turn and ended up in a dead-end alley in a notorious gang area. Members of the "Avenue" gang showered the car with gunshots, killing a 3-year-old girl inside named Stephanie Kuhen and wounding her stepfather and baby brother. The gang members responsible for the shooting were arrested, and they are all now serving long prison sentences for their crimes.

Even if someone carries a knife for protection, he or she is more likely to use it in a fight and may end up injuring an innocent person.

In the media

Gangs have reputations for violence, which they want to protect in order to rule with fear. If anyone challenges a gang member, the gang takes revenge. This may include beating up the person or harming their family. In the United States, in 2003, Brenda Paz, a 17-year-old girl, was killed for talking to the police about the Maras Salvatrucha. Four of her friends were later convicted of her murder. In 2006, Ernesto "Smokey" Miranda, one of the founders of Maras Salvatrucha, was murdered after deciding not to attend a party for a gang member who had just been released from prison. He had reformed and had been working to help keep children out of gangs.

Are gangs racist?

When a black person is stabbed by a white person, or a white person is stabbed by a black person, certain questions immediately arise—was the attack racist or was the attack carried out for other reasons? Some gang-related attacks and knife attacks are racist but many attacks are not. It is not always easy for the police to establish if the motive for the attack was racist or if the attack was carried out for other reasons, regardless of the victim's color or race. For instance, although the victim and attacker may come from different ethnic or cultural backgrounds, they may also come from rival gangs or have been involved in arguments over drugs.

Senseless violence

"Respect" used to mean admiration or appreciation. Today, on the streets, respect means fear—and gangs want respect. They target people they believe haven't shown enough respect, who have dared to challenge them, or who ignore them. An example of this is in the death of a young man in Los Angeles in 2008. Jamiel Andre Shaw—just 17—was on his way home when two men pulled up in a car. They asked which gang he belonged to, but Jamiel didn't reply. The men shot and killed him. Jamiel was not a gang member. The killers have not yet been found.

Chapter 4

Why do people get involved in gangs and knife crime?

Some people are forced into joining a gang; others choose to join because they think it provides a way out of a life of poverty. A gang may seem to offer a sense of belonging to young people who do not have a strong family unit. Some people join because they are influenced by other family members or friends who are in gangs. New recruits often think that gang life will bring riches and power, but the reality can be a bleak life of crime, violence, and fear.

Bullied into joining

Some gangs pressure people to become involved. Perhaps a young person has spent time with a particular group for a while and then is suddenly put under pressure to join in a criminal activity. Gangs often have profiles on networking websites such as Myspace or Bebo and use Internet chatrooms and text messages to intimidate and pressure people into joining them. Gangs sometimes target and threaten local people with a clear message—join the gang or live in fear of it.

Who joins?

Gangs often recruit new members, both boys and girls, from schools, because younger people are more impressionable than adults. Gang members come from all ethnic groups, but some gangs are characterized by belonging to a certain ethnic group.

Joining a gang may seem like a way out for young people living in deprived areas, but the reality is often very different.

Gangs often recruit new members by intimidation, threatening to attack them or their families unless they join the gang.

Once a person has joined a gang, it can be difficult for him or her to leave because of pressure and threats from other gang members.

Although it is very hard for young people to resist the pressure to join gangs, there are many support organizations to help them. It's not easy to stand up to such pressure and walk away. However, if you find yourself being pushed into joining a gang, talk to an adult you trust or contact one of the many confidential organizations and support services that help young people walk away from gangs. It's important, too, to stand up for what you believe in and for your hopes for the future.

FACTS

Common reasons why a young person turns to crime are:

* Lack of education and missing schooling.

* Poor family relationships.

* Peer pressure—having friends who commit crimes.

* Having family members who commit crimes.

Family breakup

Some people believe that the rise in gang and knife crime is a result of poor parenting. They think that a lack of rules and discipline within the family means that a young person will not follow laws and will not respect other people. Some people also believe that if a child comes from a violent and abusive home, it is likely that he or she will follow a violent and abusive pattern of behavior.

Family breakup is common and there is much discussion in the media about the effect of family breakdown on young people. In the United States, 26% of young people under the age of 21 live in single-parent families, usually brought up by their mother. If a young person feels no bond or support with his or her family, and no sense of belonging, a gang might seem to offer this.

Some people argue that without a father as a role model, children are more likely to get into trouble, especially in the case of boys.

Looking for a family

New recruits to gangs often come from unhappy, troubled homes. To the recruit, the gang might seem to offer the security and sense of belonging that should come from a family. But the reality of gang membership is belonging to a group that may turn on you, that thrives only on threats and violence, and from which it is very difficult to escape.

Keeping it in the family

Young people often look up to and admire older brothers and sisters or cousins. If they are involved in gangs or crime, their younger relations might want to copy their behavior. The older brothers and sisters might boast about their power on the streets or how much money they make from their crimes. Younger relations could easily be influenced by their boasts and join a life of crime, danger, and violence. It's important to remember that gang members usually exaggerate their power. They also do not brag about the reality of gang life, such as suffering beatings and attacks from rival gangs and maybe their own gang members, too.

No money, no jobs

Many gangs operate in deprived areas, where there is little to do, few jobs, and where people have very little money. Gangs can make members feel special, different, and exclusive, offering young people a way out from a life of unemployment and poverty. Gang leaders may seem to have a lot of money and wear expensive clothing and jewelry. This might attract young people to the gang and encourage them to join it. However, most gang members themselves do not become rich, but instead become caught up in a world of violence.

It happened to me

"I never really felt I belonged at school. And I never really had a home like other kids. Joining a crew felt like belonging somewhere. For the first time in my life, I felt like I had people looking out for me. They were my brothers and I felt important. But when we got involved in some serious trouble, and started doing really bad things, it all turned nasty. I couldn't rely on them for support. I realized they weren't my family. I was lucky, I got out."

Rami, age 16.

What's to blame?

With every fatal stabbing, people wonder why so many innocent people are harmed and even killed in such a senseless way. There is much debate about why young people turn to violence and gang culture, and what kind of society creates a culture where knives are used to resolve minor arguments and disagreements. Some people think too much attention is given to understanding why a person behaves in a violent way. They think that the focus should be on the punishment, and that if young people knew they could not avoid punishment, they would correct their behavior. However, once they are part of a gang, young people may feel they have to commit crimes—the punishment they will receive from their gang if they do not may seem worse than being arrested and sentenced.

Cultural influences

Gang culture is often glamorized in movies and music, with members shown dripping in expensive jewelry and living the life of a celebrity. But movies and music rarely portray the other side to gang culture—the drug addiction, the fear, distress, and death the gang causes.

Some people think that images of gang culture and violence in movies and some music influence young people to copy aggressive behavior.

Some famous rappers and hip hop artists have been involved in gangs, and violence has often broken out at their concerts. Several rappers, including Tupac Shakur, have been killed in what many believe is gang warfare. Some people believe that the lifestyle and lyrics in rap and hip hop music, often about violence, gang wars, and drugs, promote aggressive behavior and encourage gang membership. They argue that young people need more positive role models. However, others think it is unfair to blame the words in music for the rise in gang culture and violence, and they argue that the lyrics simply reflect the reality of living on the street in poor neighborhoods.

Real violence

Many people enjoy playing computer and video games. But some games promote images and actions of violence and aggression. Research shows that children and young people exposed to this violence become numb to the effects of violence in the real world. This may have an influence on their behavior away from a computer or video screen.

Many people think violent games affect the way that young people behave in real life.

* Do you think that the violence associated with some musicians is responsible for the rise in gang and knife crime?

* Do you think individuals are completely responsible for their behavior, or does society play a part in shaping how an individual behaves?

* How do you think understanding why people turn to crime can help to reduce violent behavior?

The myth and the reality

To a young girl or boy who has had little education and who comes from a troubled home, a gang may appear to be an alternative family and future. Gang members may wear expensive jewelry and drive expensive cars. They give the impression that being in a gang offers protection and a way of making money from criminal activities. The reality is much more stark and brutal.

A life of danger

Some young people think that belonging to a gang makes them powerful and protects them on the streets, but belonging to a gang makes every member a target for rival gang members who want to prove that their gang is more ruthless and more powerful than any other.

DOs & DON'Ts

✳ **Do think about the reality of gang life.**

✳ **Don't believe you will be safer in a gang.**

✳ **Do go to an adult you really trust to help you stay away from gangs.**

✳ **Do think about your future and your hopes. Will gang membership really help you achieve your dreams and goals?**

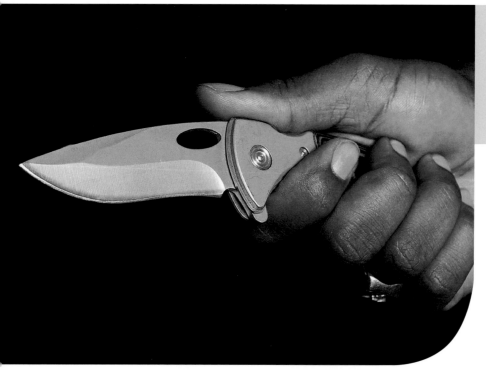

A person who carries a knife isn't cool and will end up in prison if he or she is caught.

Knives don't protect you

Being in a gang traps people in a world of fear and violence.

Many young people carry knives for protection, never intending to use them. However, the facts show that weapons don't offer protection. In the United States, there is evidence that criminals often attack police with the police's own weapons.

People who carry knives for protection are likely to use them and might end up killing someone. This could lead to a prison sentence, even if the person was acting in self-defense. Carrying a knife doesn't offer protection, it creates a false sense of security. There is always the chance that an attacker might grab the knife and use it against the person who is carrying it.

Getting out

Gangs threaten and pressure members to remain in the gang, because without members, the gang weakens. There are ways to leave if you have become involved in a gang. Stay positive and don't try to deal with the problem on your own. The first thing to do is to talk to your parents or guardians, or an adult you trust.

Chapter 5

The effects of gang and knife crime

If a victim of a knife crime is lucky enough to survive an injury, the wound will heal in time, but there are often longer-lasting effects on the individual and his or her family. Victims often suffer from fear and panic for a long time after any attack.

As well as the victim, gang and knife crime causes long-term emotional damage to family and friends.

It happened to me

"I will never forget what happened to one young man. He was stabbed in his buttock. The blade tore into a blood vessel, which caused massive internal bleeding. He was only 15 years old, with his whole life ahead of him. Apparently, he had been carrying a knife on a night out—and the knife was turned against him in a fight. His mother was waiting for him to come home. Instead, she received a call from the police and last saw her son dying in a pool of blood."

Samuel Warne, surgeon.

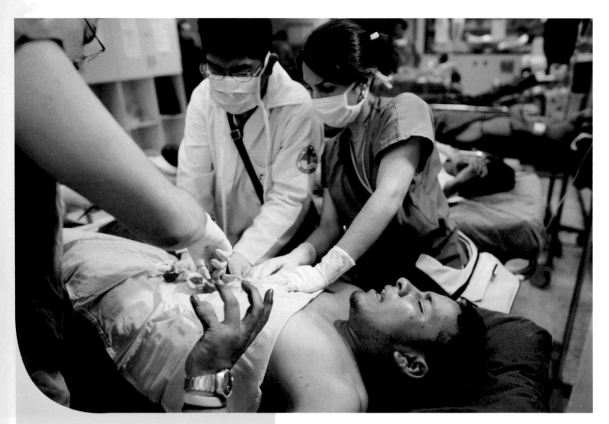

Stabbing attacks destroy the lives of many young people.

Stab wounds

Any knife wound can kill. There is no safe part of the body to stab someone. A stab anywhere on the body can be fatal: the knife may pierce a vital organ, such as the liver or heart, or some other body part, causing serious injury. Even a stab wound in the buttocks can sever an artery and kill a person within six minutes unless he or she receives medical treatment.

Even if the victim recovers from the stabbing, he or she may be left with disfiguring scars—a constant reminder of the attack. Then there are the psychological scars—many victims feel too scared to go out on their own and enjoy their lives again.

FACTS

A knife victim will lose half of their blood within 30 minutes. Unless they receive medical help, for every minute after they have been stabbed, their chance of survival decreases by 10%. Sometimes a victim survives, but can be left brain-damaged or paralyzed because of blood loss or nerve damage.

How it feels for families

A fatal stabbing destroys the life of the victim, but also affects the lives of the victim's family. The loss of a person's life can devastate his or her friends and family—parents, brothers and sisters, aunts and uncles.

Even if an attacker only intends to carry a knife for safety, but then uses it in self-defense, he or she will probably end up in prison. The effect on his or her family will also be devastating. They will have to live with the fact that their child killed or seriously injured someone else, and they will only be able to visit their child in prison.

In the media

In 2008, David Idowu, age 14, was stabbed as he walked across a park in London on his way to play soccer. He died from his injuries. A 16-year-old boy was later convicted of his murder. David's mother said that David had simply crossed the park to play soccer with his brother—and as a result, he became yet another innocent victim of knife crime.

The fatal stabbing of a young person can destroy the lives of the victim's family and friends.

TALK ABOUT

* How would you feel if your brother, sister, mom, dad, or best friend was stabbed?

* How would you feel if someone close to you seriously injured or killed another human being?

Living in fear

Some people live in fear. Perhaps they have previously been threatened or attacked with a knife, or followed by a gang. Their fear may stop them from going out and they may feel very unhappy and isolated.

Not all crimes are reported to the police. Sometimes, people don't want police coming to their home, because they fear that gang members will frighten them in an attempt to prevent them giving evidence to the police.

Parents or guardians may be fearful for their children and may want to keep them safe at home. This can lead to tensions, especially when young people want to go out. Parents will feel more confident about their children's wellbeing if they are reassured by them that they have taken measures to stay safe.

The victims of gang violence are often too frightened to leave their own homes.

Chapter 6

What does the law say?

There are laws to stop gangs committing criminal activity. For example, it is illegal for a person to carry a knife if he or she intends to use it as a weapon, even if the knife doesn't belong to them. Punishments for crimes committed by gang members are sometimes more severe than they would be for an individual acting alone.

The consequences of carrying a knife

In some countries, a school principal has the right to search a pupil at school for a knife, or to give permission for a teacher to do so. The police can search any person of any age for a knife. If someone is found with a knife, even if they only carry it for protection, they can be taken to a police station and arrested. They might go to court and have to face a judge who will sentence them. It is likely that they will be punished for the crime.

Carrying a knife is a criminal offense in many countries and can result in a lengthy prison sentence.

Anyone who is with a friend who uses a knife to attack another person could also be charged with murder if the victim dies. They will be sent to prison for a long time. They may not be the attacker, but the fact that they were with their friend who is, makes them guilty of participating in the crime.

Laws

Each country has its own laws regarding carrying knives. However, it is illegal to use any weapon to harm someone else, and to carry one with the intent to do so. Countries have different rules about the punishments for crimes committed by young people. In general, people 14–16 years old who are found guilty are likely to go a young offenders' institution. Younger children are more likely to be placed under the supervision and care of social workers.

Whatever their age, courts will punish young people for carrying and using knives.

FACTS

The age of criminal responsibility is the age at which you can be held responsible for a crime. In England and Wales, the age of criminal responsibility is 10. In the United States, it varies from state to state between the ages of 6 and 12. In Canada, it is 12 and in France, it is 17.

Caught

In many countries, if a young person is caught carrying a knife, it is likely that he or she will be taken to a police station. Police can take a young person to the police station without telling their parents or guardians. However, an adult must be present when a young person over the age of 10 is questioned by the police.

At the police station

The police will take fingerprints and empty the offender's pocket. Parents or guardians are contacted and asked to come to the station. When they arrive, the offender will be questioned about why he or she is carrying a knife.

Sometimes, the police will issue a caution. This is an official warning noted on police records. Most young people caught with knives are sent to court, even if the knife has not been used. If the person is found guilty, he or she will be punished. In some countries, the offender will also get a criminal record. Young people found guilty of knife crime may be sent to a young offenders' institution. This punishment may even be given to a person who was only carrying the knife for protection.

Being in prison or a young offenders' institution means being locked up and having very little contact with family or friends.

It happened to me

"I'd been out with some friends. We'd come across trouble before, and this time, I thought I'd take a knife, just to scare anyone if they tried to threaten me. But we were searched by the police. They found my knife and took me to the police station. It was really scary. Dad came down and was so shocked at what I'd done. My case went to court and I've now got a criminal record, which means I can't study to be a doctor when I leave school. All that for carrying a knife."

Joe, age 16.

DOs & DON'Ts

If you are called to court to give evidence against someone else:

✱ **Don't try to cover up what you saw. It is illegal to do so and you should always be honest.**

✱ **Do tell police officers, social workers, or court workers if you are worried about your safety.**

Sentencing

A judge decides the sentence by taking into consideration why the offender carried the knife, what type of knife it was, and if he or she has a criminal record. If the offender used the knife against someone, the punishment will be custodial. This means being locked up in a young offenders' institution or in a prison.

Giving evidence

People who witness a knife or gang attack may be asked to give evidence in court. This might mean giving evidence against a friend. This is hard to do, but it is vital that evidence is given against people who use knives or are violent gang members.

Some people might be afraid to give evidence against another person because of fear of retaliation. Officials in courts are specially trained to help young people feel safe and confident about giving evidence. Evidence can be given behind screens, or via video links, so the witness cannot be seen, and cannot see the suspect, in court.

A criminal record

Most job application forms ask if the applicant has a criminal record. If they do, it will close the door to many jobs. A person with a criminal record often cannot work with children and they cannot join the police or the army. Some professions, such as medicine, dentistry, and nursing, are not open to people with criminal records. A criminal record can mean that someone is not allowed to travel to some foreign countries. In years to come, that might mean missing out on a great vacation or a fantastic job opportunity abroad.

A criminal record may make foreign vacations and traveling overseas impossible for several years.

DOs & DON'Ts

* Don't carry a knife—even if it makes you feel safer.

* Don't think you can carry a knife for your own safety—it is still illegal.

* Do tell your parents or guardians about any worries you have for your safety.

* Don't hang around with other people who carry knives—if they use them, you will find yourself involved in the trouble, too.

If you know someone has used a knife against someone else:

* Don't keep it to yourself. Tell an adult you trust.

* Do be aware that your friend might attack someone else.

* Do be aware that if you are present when a stabbing takes place, you could be prosecuted as an accomplice, too.

Hurting your family

The potential consequences of carrying a knife and being part of a gang are enormous. If a young person is caught carrying a knife or being involved in gang violence, his or her parents will be asked to go to the police station. The young person may have to go to court. If he or she is found guilty, the young person will be given a criminal record and may even end up in a young offenders' institution.

It is very likely that parents or guardians will be shocked and extremely upset. They may find it difficult to trust their child in the same way again. If the parents or guardians consider a friend to be a bad influence, they may not allow him or her to see their child. There is always the danger, too, that younger brothers and sisters might be influenced by the offender's behavior and join a gang or start to carry a knife.

Think about the consequences for the rest of your family if you are caught carrying a knife.

Chapter 7

Can we stop gangs and knife crime?

Many young people who have lost someone to a fatal stabbing are speaking out against knife crime. Former gang members are also taking a stand against knife and gang crime. One of the founders of the Crips gang, Stanley "Tookie" Williams, turned his back on gang life while he was in prison. He wrote books for children that spoke out against gangs. However, despite attempts to have his death sentence overturned, Williams was executed in 2005.

In his books, Williams spoke openly about his experiences as a gang member in the hope that his story would discourage young people from joining gangs.

Breaking the cycle

One seven-year study showed that Alice Springs in Australia was the stabbing capital of the world, with 200 operations carried out on stabbing victims each year. Increased policing and alcohol controls have reduced the number of stabbings dramatically.

It happened to me

"My brother was in a gang. I used to really admire him, and think he was so cool. He always stood up for me. I wanted to follow what he did. But now my brother is in a wheelchair. He was stabbed by a member of his own gang after some silly argument. Was it worth it?"

Hannah, age 14.

Increasing awareness of the dangers can help. In several states in the United States, former gang members, victims of gang crimes and their families, and members of the local community who are tired of being threatened by gangs, march through their neighborhood in a show of strength against gangs. If more people speak out against gangs, young people will find gang life less attractive.

Breaking the cycle

In many cities in Guatemala, South America, there is a problem with violent street gangs. The gangs are made up of young people who are caught in a cycle of poverty, drug-taking, and crime. Several years ago, the cycle was broken for some gang members. A music theater project called Iqui Balam brought together members of rival gangs to share their experiences, rather than fight each other. Bringing together rival gangs was not easy—it took patient and sensitive negotiation with gang leaders to allow gang members to take part. Today, the group runs many projects, including using rap music to promote messages of peace and education, and graffiti competitions.

The family of knife victim Ben Kinsella, from London, campaign to make young people aware of the dangers of carrying knives.

Deterring young people from gangs and knife crime

It is often the case that many young people who end up in trouble with gangs or prosecuted for knife crime come from unhappy homes. These young people often have no positive role models, no supportive family, and very little money. Some people think that giving them support, understanding, and a positive outlet for their behavior will help them to stay away from gangs and knife culture. However, others think this attitude is too soft, and focuses on supporting the criminal rather than the victim.

Some people argue that longer prison sentences for gang violence and knife-related crimes are the best deterrent. Others think that the violence is often carried out on impulse, when a person is drunk or has taken illegal drugs, or when he or she is in a rage. In these situations, it is unlikely that an attacker will stop to consider the possible consequences of using a knife. However, he or she may have considered the consequences of carrying a knife before leaving home, and took it out anyway.

Hearing it from a gang

Former members of so-called Jamaican "Yardie" gangs spoke to youngsters to try to stop them copying the violent behavior of Yardie gangs. Several killings in Jamaican cities were thought to be the result of "turf wars" between different gangs. The Jamaican youths, who now belong to the Kingston Area Youth Foundation (an organization that promotes theater and arts activities for young people), have left their life of gangs to pursue successful and rewarding careers. Before this, they were caught up in a world of poverty, crime, drugs, and danger.

FACTS

In 1990 in Boston, Massachusetts, 153 people were murdered. In 1998, the number was down to 38. The fall in the murder rate was the result of a police scheme called Operation Ceasefire. The Boston police, working with church and community leaders, brought gang members together for a meeting. They told them the cycle of violence and murder in gangs had to stop. They offered support to those wanting to return to education or to pursue careers and to leave gang crime. But those who continued a life of crime and violence were told they would be pursued and face the most severe punishments. Currently, the police in Glasgow, Scotland, are using the Boston operation as inspiration for their policing tactics to reduce gang crime.

Amnesty

The police have responded to the dramatic rise in crimes involving knives and other weapons by organizing amnesties. These are opportunities for people to hand in weapons at police stations, without facing any criminal consequences. It is their chance to literally walk away from knives, and it gives the police the chance to get them off the street. Although these amnesties get knives off the streets, some people argue that it does not offer a long-term solution to making the streets safer. Knives are so easy to obtain that young people can easily replace them.

From penknives to kitchen knives, amnesties offer a chance to hand in knives that may be used as weapons.

School

Many young people who carry knives and are at risk of being hurt by a knife are at school or college. Some schools have metal detectors at the entrances to catch pupils bringing knives into school. However, many people think that if pupils feel safe, they will not feel the need to carry a knife at school. They believe it is more effective to teach children about the dangers of knives and becoming involved with gangs.

Young people who join gangs often have a difficult time at school and may end up leaving without a diploma. Given encouragement from teachers, parents, and guardians, they may start to take an interest in school and gain the skills that they will need to enjoy a successful career.

TALK ABOUT

✳ **How do you think we can tackle the problem of gang and knife crime?**

✳ **Is it better to help people turn away from crime, or to concentrate on the victims?**

✳ **Do you think that there would be a reduction in gang violence and knife crime if people knew they were likely to be caught and receive a harsh punishment?**

Education offers young people a positive alternative to gangs and knife crime.

It happened to me

"I used to be in a gang and I carried a knife because it made me feel safe and important. Then I found out about a boxing club near where I live. I started going for a laugh, but when I got into it and started training hard, I felt really good. Knowing how to box and defend myself without a knife made me feel really confident. I don't carry a knife any more, and I don't hang around with my old gang either."

Kevin, age 16.

Alternatives to violence

People lash out when they are angry. If they are carrying a knife, they are more likely to use it. Some young people are offered counseling to deal with their anger. This has been shown to reduce the number of violent attacks.

If young people wander the streets with nothing to do, they are more likely to get into trouble. Sometimes joining youth clubs or sports groups helps people find a new direction and a safe and positive outlet for their feelings.

The British singer Estelle has regularly spoken out about knife crime.

Chapter 8

Staying safe

You might have been told by your parents or guardians that it is safer to walk to and from school with a few friends rather than on your own. An individual alone often feels more vulnerable to threats or attacks. Young people might come together in groups to protect themselves, but unfortunately, this can instead attract unwelcome attention from other gangs.

Don't live in fear

The headlines rarely report good news—it doesn't sell newspapers and it doesn't grab our attention. But most people, young and old, are good, kind, and thoughtful. The streets of your town or city are generally safe. It's important to remember that, and not to live in fear.

Avoid confrontation when you are with your friends. It's not a sign of weakness, but it will keep you all safe.

Drinking and drugs

Arguments and violence are more common when people have been drinking alcohol and taking drugs. Both alcohol and illegal drugs affect someone's ability to think clearly and to consider the consequences of their actions. A person who is drunk or high on drugs is more likely to fight back when they are taunted by a gang or threatened by an individual with a knife. Gang members are often more violent when they are drunk or high on drugs, because they have less control over their behavior.

Drinking alcohol and being high on drugs makes people more aggressive, less able to protect themselves, and more likely to take risks. It is very easy for young people to feel pressured into doing things that could lead to difficult situations and trouble. So-called friends might make fun of someone for not drinking, or for not joining in when others are taking drugs. It is not worth taking unnecessary risks just to be one of the crowd.

Some young people who get involved in fights and use a knife have been drinking or taking drugs.

DOs & DON'Ts

❋ **Do hand your cell phone or wallet over if someone threatens you at knifepoint. It is unfair, and it is wrong that someone else can take what is yours in this way, but it is better to lose your phone than to get hurt.**

❋ **Don't feel it's a sign of weakness to give attackers your possessions.**

❋ **Do tell your parents or guardians and the police what has happened; if they don't know, they can't find your attackers and can't offer you the support you might need.**

Talk

If you are threatened or bullied by a gang or individual, tell an adult you trust. It's not your fault, it doesn't mean you are weak, and telling someone won't make the situation worse. It is lonely and frightening to worry about such a situation without asking someone for support. Even if you've been mugged or threatened while you were out somewhere you weren't supposed to be, or doing something your parents didn't know about, tell your parents or guardians. It is much more important that they know about your safety.

DOs & DON'Ts

If you do hang out with a large group of friends, make sure you don't frighten other people or become regarded as a threatening gang.

✳ Do let your parents or guardians know where you are and who you are with.

✳ Don't get involved in a shouting contest, because it may lead to a fight.

✳ Do tell your friends if you think they are being too aggressive.

✳ Don't shout or behave in a way that others might find threatening.

TALK ABOUT

* How has this book
  made you think
  more about the
  issues to do
  with gang and
  knife crime?

*There is nothing wrong
with hanging out with
your friends if you are just
enjoying yourselves and
not causing trouble.*

Around town

When you are going out, think ahead and plan your
trip. Try to avoid deserted areas or areas where
the street lighting is poor, especially after dark. Avoid
walking alone at night altogether. Wearing headphones
makes it harder to be aware of what's going on around
you, and it's important to stay alert. Always keep your
cell phone and wallet or purse out of sight. Even if
someone teases you, avoid confrontation. Walk away
if you can. If you are being followed, knock on a nearby
door and ask the people to call the police. You could
even go to a self-defense class, so you can protect
yourself effectively and safely.

Glossary

age of criminal responsibility The age when a person is legally responsible for their behavior and can be found guilty in a court.

amnesty A period of time during which people can admit to something that is not permitted, without being punished.

antisocial A word that describes people who are unpleasant or aggressive.

Bloods An organized gang that operates in the United States. The Crips gang is their main rival.

convicted When a person is found guilty in a court.

court A place where a judge hears evidence about a crime and decides if a person is guilty.

criminal record A list of past crimes committed by an individual.

Crips An organized gang that operates in the United States. It is the rival of the Bloods gang.

culture The attitudes and behavior within a group of people.

deprived Poor.

deter Put off.

drug trafficking The manufacture, smuggling, distribution, and selling of illegal drugs.

evidence Proof. When a person gives evidence, they explain what happened.

fatal Causing death.

graffiti Images and words painted on walls in public places.

Hells Angels A biker gang that carries out crimes throughout the United States and Canada and elsewhere in the world.

hierarchy A social order in which some people are more important than others.

immigrant Someone who has traveled to another country to live there.

intimidate To threaten and bully.

Mara Salvatrucha A widespread criminal gang that operates throughout South America and the United States.

mugging The violent robbery of an individual.

penalty Punishment.

retaliation Harming someone as revenge for an earlier act of violence.

self-defense Defending yourself from an attack from another person.

social worker A person who is trained to help support individuals and families who are experiencing difficulties.

turf An area dominated by a particular gang.

turf war A fight between different gangs to gain and control territory.

vandalize To deliberately damage someone else's property.

Further Information and Web Sites

Notes for Teachers:

The Talk About panels are to be used to encourage debate and avoid the polarization of views. One way of doing this is to use "continuum lines." Think of a range of statements or opinions about the topics that can then be considered by the pupils. An imaginary line is constructed that pupils can stand along to show what they feel in response to each statement (please see above). If they strongly agree or disagree with the viewpoint, they can stand by the signs, if the response is somewhere in between, they stand along the line in the relevant place. If the response is "neither agree, nor disagree" or they "don't know," then they stand at an equal distance from each sign, in the middle. Alternatively, continuum lines can be drawn on paper and pupils can mark a cross on the line to reflect their views.

Books to read

Gangs and Weapons
Stanley Tookie Williams
(Damamli Publishing Company, 2008)

How Can Gang Violence Be Prevented
Christi Watkins
(Greenhaven Press, 2006)

Making Smart Choices About Violence, Gangs, and Bullying
Matt Monteverd
(Rosen Central, 2008)

Web Sites

Due to the changing nature of Internet links, Rosen Publishing has developed an online list of Web sites related to the subject of this book. This site is regularly updated. Please use this link to access this list:
http://www.rosenlinks.com/act/gangs

Index

Entries in **bold** are for pictures.